Learning Short-take®

LISTEN AND BE LISTENED TO

Transform communication in a world of distraction

CATHERINE MATTISKE

TPC - The Performance Company Pty Ltd
Level 20, Darling Park
Tower 2, 201 Sussex Street,
Sydney NSW 2000
Australia

ACN 077 455 273
email: tpc@tpc.net.au
Website: www.catherinemattiske.com

© TPC – The Performance Company Pty Limited
First edition published in 2006
Second edition published in 2018
Third edition published in 2022

All rights reserved. Apart from any fair dealing for the purposes of study, research or review, as permitted under Australian copyright law, no part of this publication may be reproduced by any means without the written permission of the copyright owner. Every effort has been made to obtain permission relating to information reproduced in this publication.

The information in this publication is based on the current state of commercial and industry practice, applicable legislation, general law and the general circumstances as at the date of publication. No person shall rely on any of the contents of this publication and the publisher and the author expressly exclude all liability for direct and indirect loss suffered by any person resulting in any way from the use of or reliance on this publication or any part of it. Any options and advice are offered solely in pursuance of the author's and the publisher's intention to provide information, and have not been specifically sought.

For eBook version: By payment of the required fees, you have been granted the non-exclusive, non-transferable right to access and read the text of this e-book on screen. No part of this text may be reproduced, transmitted, downloaded, decompiled, reverse engineered, or stored in or introduced into any information storage retrieval system, in any form or by any means, whether electronic or mechanical, now known or hereinafter invented, without the express permission of the author.

A catalogue record for this book is available from the National Library of Australia

National Library of Australia
Cataloguing-in-Publication data

Mattiske, Catherine
Listen and Be Listened To: Transform communication in a world of distraction

ISBN 978-1-921547-13-3

1. Occupational training 2. Learning I. Title

370.113

Distributed by TPC - The Performance Company - www.catherinemattiske.com
For further information contact TPC - The Performance Company, Sydney Australia on +61 (02) 9555 1953.

HELLO.

Welcome to the Learning Short-take® process!

This Learning Short-take® is a bite sized learning package that aims to improve your skills and provide you with an opportunity for personal and professional development to achieve success in your role.

This Learning Short-take® combines self study with workplace activities in a unique learning system to keep you motivated and energized.
So let's get started!

Step 1:
What's inside?

- Learning Short-take®. This section contains all of the learning content and will guide you through the learning process.
- Learning Activities. You will be prompted to complete these as you read through.
- Learning Journal. This is a summary of your key learnings.
  Update it when prompted.
- Skill Development Action Plan. Learning is about taking action. This is your action plan where you'll plan how you will implement your learning.

Step 2:
Complete the Learning Short-take®

- Learning Short-takes® are best completed in a quiet environment that is free of distractions.
- Schedule time in your calendar to complete the Learning Short-take® and prioritize this time as an investment in your own professional development.
- Depending on the title, most participants complete the Learning Short-take® from 90 minutes to 2.5 hours.

Step 3:
Meet with your Manager/Coach

- Schedule a 30 minute meeting with your Manager or Coach.
- At this meeting share your completed Activities, Learning Journal and Skill Development Action Plan.
- Most importantly, discuss and agree on how you will implement your learning in your role.

GET VIP ACCESS TO YOUR MATERIALS

This Learning Short-take® includes an interactive activity book, associated tools and job aids, plus a bonus eBook.

1 Visit https://www.catherinemattiske.com/books

2 Select your book

3 Click: VIP ACCESS

4 Enter the code: LBL2022228

WELCOME

Listen and Be Listened To
Transform communication in a world of distraction

Listen and Be Listened To combines self-study with realistic workplace activities to provide you with the key skills and techniques of effective and enhanced listening. You will learn to build more effective work relationships with your co-workers and leaders by tuning into key communication messages and responding appropriately. You will learn tips, tricks and techniques to boost active listening capability and discover that effective listening helps command respect from both the speakers and listeners point of view.

Our unique view of the world and personal style - based on our values, beliefs, attitudes and behaviors - affects how we act, perceive information, and communicate with others. It also influences the way we listen and how others listen to us. When we expect to hear certain things, we may pay attention to only what interests us. Our perception about a person, situation or subject influences our reception of information, and how much attention we choose to pay. **Listen and Be Listened To** breaks down the art and skill of active listening which is critical to building and maintaining effective working relationships.

Listen and Be Listened To includes an impactful **'Listening Tips' Job Aid**, provided to you as a free download.

Now let's get started!

1	Learning Short-take® > Start here
2	Learning Journal 63
3	Skill Development Action Plan 69
4	Quick Reference 75
5	Next Steps 89

"Speech is a joint game between the talker and the listener against the forces of confusion. Unless both make the effort, interpersonal communication is quite hopeless."

NORBERT WEINER

> "I guess I've spent my life listening to what wasn't being said."
>
> ELI KHAMAROV

Section 1

LEARNING SHORT-TAKE®

WHAT'S IN THIS LEARNING SHORT-TAKE®

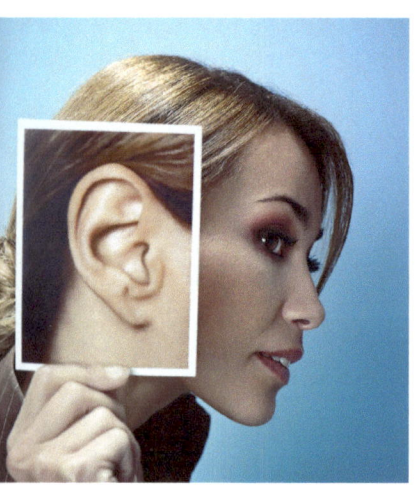

"Listening is an important component in how people judge communicative competence in the workplace."

HAAS & ARNOLD, 1995

Table of Contents

How to Complete Your Learning Short-take®	5
Activity Checklist	6
Learning Objectives	7
Let's Get Started	8
Part 1 - Listening & Communication	9
What is Listening?	10
Why Don't We Listen?	11
Corporate Communication Theory	15
Listening to Non-Verbal Communication	20
Part 2 - Listening Barriers	27
Listening Power	28
Listening Roadblocks	30
Specific Listening Barriers	33
Portrait of a Poor Listener	36
Part 3 - Listening Styles	39
Effective Communication	40
Individual Listening Styles	41
Diverted Listening Styles	44
Listening Approaches	47
Part 4 - Active Listening	51
The Art of Active Listening	52
8 Strategies for Active Listening	53
Part 5 - Top Tips for Effective Listening	59

HOW TO COMPLETE YOUR LEARNING SHORT-TAKE®

1. **Reflect on your skills and abilities** in active listening, and how well you use this skill to achieve success in your role.
2. **Complete the Activities as directed.**
3. **Highlight specific skill areas** that you believe you could develop more. Add these to the Learning Journal as you proceed throughout the short-take.
4. When you have completed this Learning Short-take® **meet with your Manager/Coach**. In this meeting, you will jointly establish a personal Skill Development Action Plan.
5. **Subject to your coach's final review** and assessment, you will either sign off the module, or undertake further skill development as appropriate.

"Further, individual performance in an organization is found to be directly related to listening ability or perceived listening effectiveness."

HAAS & ARNOLD, 1995

ACTIVITY CHECKLIST

During this Learning Short-take® you will be prompted to complete the following activities:

- Activity # 1 - Initial Skills Self-Assessment 13
- Activity # 2 - True or False 19
- Activity # 3 - Listening to Non-Verbal Communication 25
- Activity # 4 - Barriers to Effective Listening 37
- Activity # 5 - Understanding Your Listening Style 48
- Activity # 6 - Managing the Listening Style of Others 50
- Activity # 7 - Quotable Quotes 57
- Activity # 8 - My Top Tips 62
- Learning Journal 63
- Skill Development Action Plan 69

"We have two ears and one mouth so that we can listen twice as much as we speak."

EPICTETUS

LEARNING OBJECTIVES

By the end of this Learning Short-take® participants should be able to:

- Define listening.
- Recognize why listening is important.
- Identify the barriers to effective listening.
- Identify their listening style and the listening style of others.
- Demonstrate techniques for active listening.
- List the tips for effective listening and identify top tips to sharpen personal listening skills
- Create a Skill Development Action Plan.

"Conversation: a vocal competition in which the one who is catching his breath is called the listener."

ANONYMOUS

LET'S GET STARTED

Each of us has a unique view of the world and a personal style based on our values, beliefs, attitudes and environment. Our style affects how we perceive information, communicate with others, and influence our behaviors. It also influences the way we listen and how others listen to us. Information that conflicts with our ideas and beliefs may simply be tuned out. Similarly, when we expect to hear certain things, we often only pay attention to what interests us. Our perception about a person, situation or subject influences our reception of the information, and how much attention we choose to pay. Listening is naturally a very selective and subjective experience.

The art of active listening is something that takes time and effort, however is critical to building and maintaining effective working relationships.

Listening Fact #1

The average person talks at a rate of about 125 – 175 words per minute, while we can listen at a rate of up to 450 words per minute.

This Learning Short-take® combines self-study with workplace activities to provide you with the key skills and techniques of effective listening. You will learn to build more effective work relationships with your co-workers and leaders by tuning into key communication messages and responding more appropriately. You will learn tips, tricks and techniques to boost active listening capability and discover the type of behavior that commands respect from both the speaker and listener point of view. The Learning Short-take® is designed for completion in approximately 90 minutes.

LISTENING & COMMUNICATION PART 1

PART 1 - LISTENING & COMMUNICATION

What is Listening?

Many of us think that listening is what we do while waiting for our turn to talk. However, listening is a far more difficult task than simply 'hearing'. Aside from breathing listening is the second most activity that humans engage in. However, most of us are not good listeners. Studies reveal that we normally operate at 25% of our listening capacity. Even where we devote full concentration to listening, we cannot listen at 100% efficiency unless the message is urgent and important enough to sustain our attention.

Effective listening skills are crucial to successful communication in the workplace, and in every situation where messages are sent and received. Good listening is an active, integrated communication skill that demands energy and expertise. To listen effectively we must hear and select information from the speaker, give it meaning, determine how we feel about it, and respond in a matter of seconds. We must also understand the speaker's purpose which influences the way we listen, and how we perceive what is said. The speaker and the listener must have the same purpose if the communication is to be effective.

In the workplace, poor listening comes at a high price. Organizations continue to spend both time and money in repeating instructions, and redoing projects and tasks that were carried out incorrectly. Of even greater concern is that many workplace accidents are the result of an individual not listening to directions or warnings prior to acting.

Why Don't We Listen?

If listening is this important, then why aren't we better at it? There is actually a physiological reason for the listening difficulties that we experience. Our capacity to listen is up to 450 words a minute, while the average speaking rate is about 125 words per minute. This gives us ample time to daydream and think about other things while someone is talking to us.

Another contributing factor to our poor listening habits is lack of training. While our school system focuses on reading, writing, and speaking, listening skills are often neglected. Even as adults we can take courses in speed-reading, business writing, and public speaking, while continuing to ignore the communication skill that we use the most - listening.

"Our brains are capable of comprehending speech at four to five times the rate at which most people can speak. So as someone else is talking, we take all that downtime and go out on mental excursions."

JACK E. HULBERT

"When I ask you to listen to me and you start giving me advice, you have not done what I asked. When I ask you to listen to me and you begin to tell me why I shouldn't feel that way, you are trampling on my feelings. When I ask you to listen to me and you feel you have to do something to solve my problem, you have failed me - strange as that may seem."

LEO BUSCAGLIA

Another reason for poor listening is that we are simply too busy to focus exclusively on another individual. Sometimes we don't listen to others because we think that they expect us to solve their problems. However, few of our colleagues or friends really want us to organize their finances, find them new mates or solve their work frustrations. Often they simply want to share their thoughts and feelings on a situation only for us to understand and appreciate what they are going through.

Complete Activity # 1
Initial Skills Self-Assessment

ACTIVITY 1: INITIAL SKILLS SELF-ASSESSMENT

Understanding how you currently listen is critical to the development of active listening behaviors and effective workplace communication. This assessment covers the key skills required to consciously listen, in order to improve communication outcomes and job success.

Rate yourself on each of the techniques.

7 is competent and confident, little need for improvement
4 is average, needs improvement
1 is uncomfortable, major need for improvement

- Note specific areas of improvement related to each skill that you would like to develop. Be sure to include your reasons for your rating in each skill, as this reasoning will be a key part of the initial goal setting session with your coach.
- Start thinking about a personal development plan and identify two or three things you could do to improve your skills in this area and write them in the space provided.

I...	Rating	Reasoning
listen for feelings, attitudes, perceptions, and values as well as for facts.	1 2 3 4 5 6 7	
try to listen for what is not said.	1 2 3 4 5 6 7	
avoid interrupting the person who is speaking to me.	1 2 3 4 5 6 7	
actually pay attention to who is speaking as opposed to 'faking' attention.	1 2 3 4 5 6 7	
refrain from 'tuning people out' because I don't like them, disagree with them, or find them dull.	1 2 3 4 5 6 7	
work hard to avoid being distracted from what is said by the speaker's style, mannerism, clothing, voice etc.	1 2 3 4 5 6 7	
make certain that the person's status has no bearing on how well I listen to him/her.	1 2 3 4 5 6 7	
avoid letting my expectations (hearing what I want to hear) determine or influence my listening behavior.	1 2 3 4 5 6 7	

ACTIVITY 1: CONTINUED

I…	Rating	Reasoning
try to read the non-verbal communication – gestures, posture, eye contact, facial expression etc to help correctly interpret the message.	1 2 3 4 5 6 7	
screen out noise and outside distractions to concentrate on the speakers message.	1 2 3 4 5 6 7	
try to 'stay with' speakers who are hard to follow ie. those who are slow in their speech or whose ideas are poorly organized.	1 2 3 4 5 6 7	
use non-verbal communication (eye contact, head nods etc) to indicate that I wish to hear more.	1 2 3 4 5 6 7	
re-state or re-phrase the other person's statements when necessary so that he/she will know that I understood.	1 2 3 4 5 6 7	
have not understood, I candidly admit to this and ask for a restatement.	1 2 3 4 5 6 7	
avoid framing my response to what is being said while the other person is still speaking.	1 2 3 4 5 6 7	
recognise that words can mean different things to different people.	1 2 3 4 5 6 7	
practice to increase my listening efficiency.	1 2 3 4 5 6 7	
take notes when necessary to help me remember.	1 2 3 4 5 6 7	
find out what words mean when they are used in a way not familiar to me.	1 2 3 4 5 6 7	
look at the person who is talking to me.	1 2 3 4 5 6 7	

Personal development plan ideas:

1

2

Now update your Learning Journal (page 63)

Corporate Communication Theory

Expressing our wants, feelings, thoughts and opinions clearly and effectively is only half of the communication process that is needed for interpersonal effectiveness. The other half is listening and understanding what others communicate to us. When a person decides to communicate with another person, they do so to fulfil a need. They either want or need something, or have feelings or thoughts about something. In deciding to communicate, the person selects the method or code that they believe will effectively deliver the message to the other person. The code used to send the message could be either verbal or nonverbal. When the other person receives the coded message, they go through the process of interpreting it into something that they understand or apply meaning to.

Effective communication exists between two people when the receiver interprets and understands the sender's message in the same way the sender intended it.

Listening Fact #2

Listening accounts for approximately 1/3 of the characteristics perceivers use to evaluate communication competence in co-workers.

Why is listening often difficult?

Listening effectively is difficult because people vary in their communication skills and in how clearly they express themselves, and often have different needs, wants and purposes for interacting.

There is a distinction between hearing the words and really listening for the message. When we listen effectively we understand what the person is thinking and/or feeling from the other person's own perspective. It is as if we were standing in the other person's shoes, seeing through their eyes and listening through their ears.

Our own viewpoint may be different and we may not necessarily agree with the person, but as we listen, we understand from the other's perspective.

Sources of Difficulty for the Speaker	Sources of Difficulty for the Listener
Using a unique code or unconventional method for delivering the message.	Being preoccupied and not listening.
Paying too much attention to how the other person is taking the message, or how the person might react.	Being so interested in what you have to say that you listen mainly to find an opening to get the floor.
Getting lost, forgetting your point or the purpose of the interaction.	Formulating and listening to your own rebuttal to what the speaker is saying.
Body language or nonverbal elements contradicting or interfering with the verbal message, such as smiling when anger or hurt is being expressed.	Listening to your own personal beliefs about what is being said.
	Evaluating and making judgments about the speaker or the message.
Voice volume too low to be heard.	Not asking for clarification when you know that you do not understand.
Making the message too complex, either by including too many unnecessary details or too many issues.	

The Three Modes of Listening

1. **Competitive Listening** happens when we are more interested in promoting our own point of view than in understanding or exploring someone else's view. Either we listen for openings to take the floor, or for flaws or weak points, we can attack. As we pretend to pay attention we are impatiently  waiting for an opening, or internally formulating our rebuttal and planning our devastating comeback that will destroy their argument and make us the victor.

2. In **Passive Listening**, we are genuinely interested in hearing and understanding the other person's point of view. We are attentive and passively listen. We assume that we heard and understand correctly, however stay passive and do not verify it.

3. **Active Listening** is the single most useful and important listening skill. In active listening we are also genuinely interested in understanding what the other person is thinking, feeling, wanting or what the message means, and we are active in checking out our understanding before we respond with our own new message. We restate or paraphrase our understanding of their message and reflect it back to the sender for verification. This verification or feedback process is what distinguishes active listening and makes it effective.

To listen effectively, we must be actively involved in the communication process, and not just listening passively. We all act and respond based on our understanding, and often there is a misunderstanding that neither of us is aware of. When actively listening, if a misunderstanding has occurred, it will be known immediately, and the communication can be clarified before any further misunderstanding occurs.

We will talk further about the techniques and benefits of **active listening** later in this Learning Short-take®.

Listening Fact #3

Listening and listening-related abilities such as understanding, open-mindedness, and supportiveness constitute the single dimension upon which people make judgments about communication competence.

Complete Activity # 2
True or False

ACTIVITY 2: TRUE OR FALSE

Taking time to reflect on listening behavior by exploring the listening habits of others is a good way to identify and overcome your own personal listening barriers. The following exercise will help you to become aware of listening barriers.

The statements listed below reflect many of the processes during communication that influence listening effectiveness. Mark each statement True or False.

T or F	Statement
	1. People tend to pay attention to what interests them.
	2. People tend to expect or anticipate what they are familiar with.
	3. Sometimes people distort things so they hear what they want to hear.
	4. Listening is a natural process.
	5. A person's training, experience, and knowledge affect what the person perceives.
	6. Hearing and listening are the same.
	7. Listening is a skill.
	8. Most people have a short attention span and have difficulty concentrating on the same thing to too long.
	9. Listening requires little energy; it is "easy".
	10. The speaker is totally responsible for the success of the communication.
	11. An effective listener keeps an open, curious mind.
	12. Speaking is a more important part of the communication process than listening.
	13. When a listener's emotional level is high, he or she will be an effective listener.
	14. When a person is involved with internal distractions, he or she will not be able to listen to what the speaker says.
	15. Being critical and judging a speaker is not an effective listening skill.

Now update your Learning Journal (page 63)

Activity # 2 - Check Your Answers:
1-T, 2-T, 3-T, 4-F, 5-T, 6-F, 7-T, 8-T, 9-F, 10-F, 11-T, 12-F, 13-F, 14-T, 15-T

Listening to Non-Verbal Communication

Professor Albert Mehrabian's communications model

Professor Albert Mehrabian has pioneered the understanding of communications since the 1960's. He received his Ph.D. from Clark University and in 1964 commenced an extended career of teaching and research at the University of California, Los Angeles.

Aside from his many and various other fascinating works, Mehrabian established this classic statistic for the effectiveness of spoken communications:

> *"Even the best communications are worthless if they fall on deaf ears."*
> RICHARD BIERCK

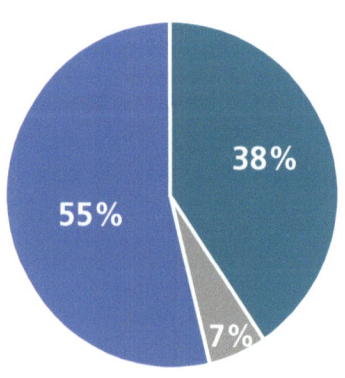

7% of meaning is in the words that are spoken

38% of meaning is paralinguistic (the way that the words are said)

55% of meaning is in facial expression

Mehrabian's model above has become one of the most widely referenced statistics in communications. The theory is particularly useful in explaining the importance of meaning, as distinct from words.

Understanding the difference between words and meaning is a vital capability for effective communications and relationships. For example, as John Ruskin so elegantly put it: "The essence of lying is in deception, not in words."

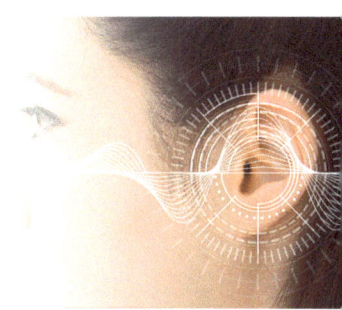

"The essence of lying is in deception, not in words."

JOHN RUSKIN, 1819-1900.

Listening to the Body Language of Others

While it may sound extreme, listening to the facial expressions of the person who is talking, can give you significant insight into the communication message. People convey a multitude of emotions via their facial expressions and these can change significantly, as the speaker discusses things they have feelings about. Movement of the lips, mouth, cheek muscles and eyebrows can provide important data about what is going on internally with the person you are listening to. Become aware of expressions that convey tension, doubt, trust, inattention etc and adapt your listening style to suit.

Listening to the emotional tone of a talker is another skill that can assist in listening to what has not been expressed verbally. Tone of voice conveys attitude and signals how to deal with a person in a particular situation. This form of communication is largely unconscious and less likely to be manipulated or disguised by the speaker.

The skilled listener hears more than the speaker's words. They listen to the pitch, rate, and volume of speech, as well as the subtle variations in tone.

"People give a lot of nonverbal messages about whether they are listening. As a rule, if they're crossing their legs, fidgeting, or looking around a lot, chances are you don't have their rapt attention."

DOE LANG

Getting Others to Listen to You

Not only is it important for you as a listener to read the body language of others, it is also important that you can engage the listener when it is your turn to speak. Most of us read body language unconsciously. When someone is fidgeting and not making eye contact, we sense that our conversation is not stimulating that person. Once identified, the wandering mind of your listener can be lured back into your discussion or conversation by using a variety of techniques.[1]

Listening Fact #4

Being more willing to communicate and less apprehensive about listening and speaking is an indicator of better listening comprehension.

[1] Richard Bierck. Are You Listening to Me?

1. Change Your Tone

A sudden pause or change in vocal tone can have the same effect on a preoccupied mind as turning off the television on a sleepy viewer: they both awaken. Speakers who use this technique successfully, follow a pause by saying something clever or insightful. To use this strategy, have something ready to say when you have the listeners' attention.

2. Ask a Question

When you suspect that the listener is taking a mental vacation from your conversation, ask them a question about the topic at hand. Asking open questions requires the listener to think and respond to your conversation in detail, giving you some insight into how well they have been listening. On the other hand, a simple 'yes' or 'no' closed question will provide immediate feedback as to whether they were listening at all. Closed questions 'pull the listener up' by forcing them to respond one way or another to your question, often when they have no idea what you were even talking about. Either way, if they weren't listening before, they are likely to start listening now.

Listening Fact #5

An individual's willingness to listen is positively correlated with communication skills and negatively related to receiver apprehension and sender based communication apprehension.

3. Tailor your Language

Again, if your listener has tendency to daydream during conversation, tailor your language to their listening style. For example, if you are speaking to someone who frequently looks to the left or up while you are speaking (and there does not appear to be anything interesting to look at in this direction), this type of behavior is attributed to people who visualize while listening.

This behavior is cross lateral in that these people are typically 'right brain' thinkers who process information using imagery. To hold their attention you will need language that is rich in metaphors so that they can associate a picture with the details of the conversation. For example, instead of saying 'eliminate the differences', try 'bridge the gap'.

On the flipside, if your listener is a 'left brain' thinker they will process information using logic and reason. These skilled listeners are literally oriented and can follow your words as though they were written. However, while these listeners look for analysis, logic and reason in your conversation, they are not immune to boredom. You will still need to keep the conversation interesting to hold their attention.

 **Complete Activity # 3**
Listening to Non-Verbal Communication

ACTIVITY 3
LISTENING TO NON-VERBAL COMMUNICATION

For each of the listening barriers identified below, develop strategies that you could implement to overcome these obstacles.

Listening Barrier	Strategies to Overcome this Barrier
Hearing what you want to hear	
Biased Listening	
Physical Barriers	
External Distractions	
Selective Interpretation	

Now update your Learning Journal (page 63)

"

"I tell you everything that is really nothing, and nothing of what is everything, do not be fooled by what I am saying. Please listen carefully and try to hear what I am not saying."

CHARLES C. FINN

LISTENING BARRIERS

PART 2

PART 2 - LISTENING BARRIERS

"Most of us have gone to a great deal of trouble to cram ourselves with facts and figures and features…so we talk too much because we desperately want other people to know how much we know."

JACK SNADER

Listening Power

Today, one of the biggest barriers to effective listening is that we equate speaking with power. Yet listening is more difficult than talking. Resistance to listening tends to be our cultural norm, where we falsely believe that speaking represents action and power, and listening represents weakness and apathy. This behavior has resulted in the belief that listening is a passive and compliant act, which puts the listener at the mercy of the speaker. However, it is important to realize that both the talker and the listener have power. When we ignore the power of listening, we do a disservice to the communication process.

Listening Fact #6

Spoken words only account for 30 -35% of the meaning. The rest is transmitted through nonverbal communication that only can be detected through visual and auditory listening.

Listening is a highly selective and subjective experience, where personal and competitive needs interfere with the effectiveness of the communication. Information that conflicts with the listener's present ideas and beliefs may simply be tuned out. When you expect to hear certain things, you don't listen to what is really said, often only paying attention to what interests you.

Your perception about a person, situation or subject influences the reception of the communication, and how much attention you choose to pay.

The more receptive you are to another person's point of view, the more you will pay attention to what they say. If your perceptions are positive and non-judgmental, you will be more receptive to what is being said, which in turn increases your interest and listening effectiveness.

Listening Fact #7

In a spoken message, 55% of the meaning is translated non-verbally, 38% is indicated by the tone of voice, while only 7% is conveyed by the words used.

Listening Roadblocks

A life filled with back-to-back commitments offers little leeway for listening. Similarly, a mind constantly buzzing with plans, dreams, schemes and anxieties is difficult to clear.

Good listening requires the temporary suspension of all unrelated thoughts - a blank canvas. In order to become an effective listener, you have to learn to manage what goes on in your own mind.

Technology, for all its glorious gifts, has erected new barriers to listening. Face-to-face meetings and telephone conversations (priceless listening opportunities) are being replaced by email and the distant, and somewhat sterile, anonymity of virtual meeting rooms and online chat or collaboration rooms.

Listening Fact #8

Both business practitioners and academics listed listening as one of the most important skills for an effective professional, yet only 1.5% of articles in business journals dealt with listening effectiveness.

9 Listening Roadblocks

1. Pseudo Listening:

Pretending to listen - may be listening to another conversation nearby, or thinking about something else.

2. Scoring Points:

Relating everything we hear to our own experience - "Oh! That's nothing. Wait till you hear what happened to me last week".

3. Mind Reading:

Predicting what the other person is really thinking. Saying to ourselves - "I bet that's not the real reason she came here".

4. Rehearsing:

Practicing what we are going to say next - preparing a clever or witty response and missing what is being said.

5. Cherry Picking:

Listening for a key piece of information then switching off. Hearing only what you want to hear.

Listening Fact #9

On average, viewers who just watched and listened to the evening news could only recall 17.2% of the content when not cued, and the cued group never exceeded 25%.

6. Filling Gaps:

Throwing in a word here and there when there is a natural pause.

7. Labeling:

Making judgments or assumptions, such as putting people into a category before hearing all the evidence - "a typical salesman" - or not listening to someone you think is a rambler.

8. Dueling:

Intervening here and there with defensive remark - "Well at least we deliver goods on time" - "You won't find us overcharging".

9. Side Stepping Sentiment:

Responding to expressions of emotion with clichés or jocular remarks - "It's not the end of the world is it?" - "Cheer up - tomorrow's another day".

Listening Fact #10

In a linear one-way listening task, when presented with a list of words, people can remember, on average, 7 items.

Specific Listening Barriers

1. Hearing What You Want to Hear

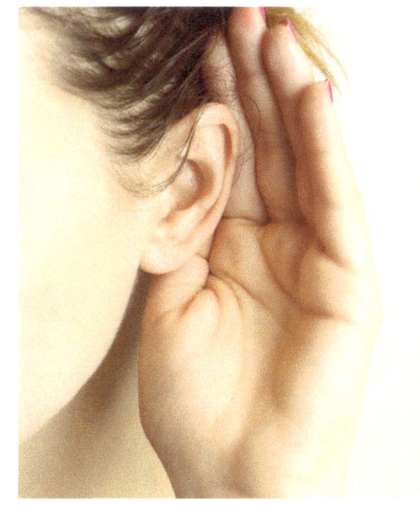

A listening barrier exists when someone hears what he or she wants to hear, not what is really communicated. This happens when one or several filters make a listener become anxious to hear something that fulfils their wishes or desires. This is a common complaint in business, particularly in a sales environment when the salesperson wants the sale to be as large as possible.

2. Biased Listening

Another block to listening occurs when we form an opinion about the value of what will be said. We label the information ahead of time as unimportant, too boring, too complex, or nothing new, and we are anxious for the speaker to get to the point.

Listening can be biased due to a negative experience we had with either the speaker, or the topic of discussion. These negative experiences are subconscious and affect our ability to listen in the 'here and now'. As a defensive measure we often tune out the talker, plan rebuttals, or formulate questions to confuse and distract the speaker.

"God gave us two ears but only one mouth. Some people say that's because he wanted us to spend twice as much time listening as talking. Other's claim it's because he knew listening was twice as hard as talking."

ANONYMOUS

3. Physical Barriers

These are things that happen to us physically which affect our ability to listen. Fatigue is a common barrier to listening, since listening takes concentration and effort. At certain times of the day, we have more energy than at others. When we feel tired or weak, it is more difficult to be attentive. This is often the case when meetings are scheduled at the end of the day or in the evenings, when attendees have already expended considerable energy getting a day's work done.

4. External Distractions

External factors can also interfere with effective listening and may include:

- The talker speaking too loudly or quietly.
- Tone of voice of the speaker.
- Loud noises such as traffic or machinery.
- Room temperatures that are too hot or too cold.
- Faulty acoustics.
- Interrupting phone calls.
- Time pressures and deadlines.

All of these factors can be a distraction and impact on our ability to listen effectively.

5. Selective Interpretation

We each have our own meanings for words because we filter them through our varied beliefs, knowledge, education, upbringing, and experience. As a result, no two people have exactly the same meaning for the same word or expression; meanings are not in words, meanings are in people. A word is simply a representation of the thing it names or describes. It is not the thing itself, and may mean something different to the speaker than it does to the listener.

"Two men were walking along a crowded sidewalk in a downtown business area. Suddenly one exclaimed, "Listen to the lovely sound of that cricket!" But the other could not hear. He asked his companion how he could detect the sound of a cricket amidst the din of people and traffic. The first man, who was a zoologist, had trained himself to listen to the voices of nature, but he did not explain. He simply took a coin out of his pocket and dropped it on the sidewalk, whereupon a dozen people began to look about them. "We hear," he said, "what we listen for."

BHAGWAN SHREE RAJNEESH -
THE DISCIPLINE OF TRANSCENDENCE

Portrait of a Poor Listener

I am one of the world's worst listeners.

I don't remember names, I interrupt, I complete other people's sentences.

I think about what I am going to say next instead of listening to what the speaker is saying now.

I am distracted by interruptions around me.

I use listening time to take a well-deserved mental vacation.

I don't ask questions, I don't paraphrase.

I really don't know if I have understood.

Complete Activity # 4
Barriers to Effective Listening

ACTIVITY 4 BARRIERS TO EFFECTIVE LISTENING

Take a few moments to examine the following pictures. Jot down the words that best describe the meaning you see in the facial expressions, body postures and gestures of each of the people in these pictures.

Now update your Learning Journal (page 63)

"

*"A good listener tries to understand what the
other person is saying.
In the end he may disagree sharply,
but because he disagrees,
he wants to know exactly what
it is he is disagreeing with."*

KENNETH A. WELLS

LISTENING STYLES

PART 3

PART 3 - LISTENING STYLES

Effective Communication

Experts estimate that people filter out or change the intended meaning of what they hear in 70 percent of communications. The biggest contributing factor to miscommunication is using a listening approach that is not appropriate either for the environment or for the message being communicated. Effective listeners consider not only their own intentions, but also the intentions of the speaker.

Because our listening styles reflect our unspoken values and motivations, we often assume that others will have listening styles that are similar to our own. Our style affects how we perceive information, communicate with others, and act. Naturally, our style also influences the way we listen and how others will listen to us. When others do not share our style, the chances of a miscommunication significantly increase.

Effective communication is much more than learning how to express our thoughts; it is also learning how to adapt our listening style in varying situations. We can do this when we know what our listening **orientation** and listening **style** is. Our listening orientation is determined by the **preferences** we assign to the communication outcome. Our listening style is the **method** of listening that comes most naturally to us. Our listening **approach** is the situational **behavior** that we demonstrate during a communication. We get into trouble when we use a listening approach that is inappropriate for the situation but in keeping with our listening orientation and listening style.

Individual Listening Styles

Barker & Watson describe four distinct approaches: people-, action-, content-, and time-oriented styles to **receiving information**. The following provides an overview of each listening style.

The People-oriented Listener

People-oriented listeners are those who show a strong **concern for others** and their **feelings**. They are external in focus, getting their energy from others and find much meaning in relationships, talking about 'we' more than 'you' or 'they'. They will seek to understand the life stories of others and use their

own personal stories as a means of understanding. They will focus on emotions, be empathetic and use appeal to emotion in their arguments. They may seem vulnerable and will use this to show that they are harmless.

People-oriented listeners can find problems when they become overly involved with others. This can impair their sense of judgment and ability to discriminate.

They may associate so strongly with others they do not see limitations and faults, and may be drawn into unwise relationships.

They also may be seen as intrusive when they seek to connect with others who are not so relationship-oriented.

The Content-oriented Listener

People who are 'Content Oriented' listeners are interested more in **what is said** rather than who is saying it or what they are feeling. They assess people more by how credible they are and will seek to test expertise and truthfulness.

They focus on facts and evidence and happily probe into detail. They are cautious in their assessment, seeking to understand cause-and-effect and sound proof before accepting anything as true. They look for both pros and cons in arguments and seek solid logical argument. They can run into trouble when they ignore the ideas and wishes of the other person and may 'throw the baby out with the bathwater', rejecting information because it does not have sufficient supporting evidence.

The Action-oriented Listener

'Action Oriented' listeners focus first on **what will be done**, what actions will happen, when and who will do them. They seek 'so what' answers in their questions and look for plans of action. They like clear, crisp descriptions and answers that are grounded in concrete reality. They like structure, bullet-points and numbered action items.

They can be impatient and hurry speakers towards conclusions. They may also be critical of people who start with the big picture and talk in ideas or concepts. This can lead them to appear overly concerned with control and less with the well-being of other people.

The Time-oriented Listener

People who are 'Time Oriented' have their eyes constantly on the clock.

They organize their day into neat compartments and will allocate time for listening, though will be very concerned if such sessions over-run.

They manage this time focus by talking about time available and seeking short answers that are to the point.

This may constrain and annoy people who are focused first on people elements and want to take as long as is needed.

Listening Fact #11

40% of individuals choose to listen with two or more distinct styles.

Diverted Listening Styles

The Biased Listener

Usually, the biased listener isn't listening. The biased listener has tuned out and is planning what to say next, based on some fixed idea already decided on regarding the topic at hand (no matter what else is said by the speaker). When bias becomes prejudice, we may even tune out a person because of his or her age, accent, or occupation.

Ask yourself: Are my biases a barrier to listening? The road to tuned-in listening begins with a deliberate effort to get rid of preconceived ideas, in order to give others a fair hearing.

The Distracted Listener

All of us fit into this category at one time or another. Distracted listeners allow internal or external distractions to prevent them from giving others their undivided attention. Unfortunately, many distracted listeners don't realize that it's important to get ready to listen.

You can't turn yourself into an attentive listener unless you make a deliberate effort to tune out internal distractions and concentrate on what the speaker is saying. If this is not possible, it may be better to set another time to meet with and listen to that person so that he or she can have your undivided attention.

For the most part, external distractions can be eliminated, by simply finding a quiet place for your important conversations, where you'll be free from interruptions.

The Impatient Listener

The impatient listener is one who interrupts and seldom lets people finish what they have to say. It can be easy to slip into this habit. If you find it extremely frustrating to listen to people who, perhaps, talk slowly, then you are probably an impatient listener.

Becoming a patient listener involves making an effort not to interrupt. At first, you'll find it difficult to listen without interrupting. However, you'll be pleasantly surprised when the lines of communication open up.

Remember, if you have been courteous enough to others, more often than not, they'll listen to you.

Listening Fact #12

People listen through one of four primary styles, including people oriented, time oriented, action oriented and content oriented. Females are more likely to be people-oriented and males are more likely to be action, content, or time oriented.

The Passive Listener

The passive listener does not realize that listening is an active process. When we are engaged in conversation with this type of listener, we are never sure if our message is understood. Why? Simply because we receive little or no feedback. Clearly, this can cause plenty of communication problems.

A telephone conversation with a passive listener is even more difficult than a face-to-face conversation. More often than not, a speaker's words are met with stony silence. That is why people often wonder if their call has been disconnected. If you are having a telephone conversation and have the person on the other line, ask "Are you still there?" it may be because you have not been communicating to him or her that you are listening.

If you have a tendency to be a passive listener, try turning yourself into a responsive listener by providing people with more feedback. Just lean slightly forward, establish eye contact, and nod or smile when appropriate. An occasional remark such as "I see," "uh-huh" or "yes" can be used when the conversation is either face-to-face (in-person or virtual) or by phone.

Listening Approaches

1. Appreciative

Listens in a relaxed manner, seeking enjoyment, entertainment, or inspiration.

2. Empathetic

Listens without judging, is supportive of the speaker and learns from the experiences of others.

3. Comprehensive

Listens to organize and make sense of information by understanding relationships among ideas.

4. Discerning

Listens to get complete information, understand the main message, and determine important details.

5. Evaluative

Listens in order to make a decision based on information provided and may accept or reject message based on personal beliefs.

 **Complete Activity # 5**
Understanding your Listening Style

 **Complete Activity # 6**
Managing the Listening Style of Others

ACTIVITY 5
UNDERSTANDING YOUR LISTENING STYLE

Take a moment to identify your **Listening Style**:
- People-oriented
- Content-oriented
- Action-oriented
- Time-oriented

Once you have identified which of the styles best describes you, answer the following questions.

What style did you identify yourself as?

Why did you identify yourself as this style?

Based on your style, what are your current strengths as a listener?

Based on your style what are your current weaknesses as a listener?

Given the information about your style, how do you plan to improve your listening? (List at least three behaviors)

1.

2.

3.

ACTIVITY 5: CONTINUED

Take a moment to identify your **Diverted Listening Style**:
- Biased Listener
- Distracted Listener
- Impatient Listener
- Passive Listener

Once you have identified which of the styles best describes you, answer the following questions.

What style did you identify yourself as?

Why did you identify yourself as this style?

Based on your style, what are your current strengths as a listener?

Based on your style what are your current weaknesses as a listener?

Given the information about your style, how do you plan to improve your listening? (List at least three behaviors)

1.

2.

3.

Now update your Learning Journal (page 63)

ACTIVITY 6
MANAGING THE LISTENING STYLE OF OTHERS

Now that you understand more about your own listening style it is important to understand the listening style of others. This will help you get maximum listening attention when communicating with a style that is different from your own.

For each of the four Listening Styles, identify what behaviors you need to demonstrate to ensure that you are being effectively listened to.

To hold the **Biased Listener's** attention I need to…

To hold the **Distracted Listener's** attention I need to…

To hold the **Impatient Listener's** attention I need to…

To hold the **Passive Listener's** attention I need to…

Now update your Learning Journal (page 63)

PART 4 - ACTIVE LISTENING

The Art of Active Listening

There is considerable effort involved in good listening. Listening requires discipline. You need to rearrange some mental furniture to make room for a conversation, and for the information it will bring. This means making time to listen. Listening is 'active' not 'passive' work. You aren't just sitting back and receiving information, you are engaged in what the other person is saying.

Research has demonstrated real physiological effects of active listening: a slight increase in heart rate and body temperature, and a rise in the body's electrical activity.[2]

"Absorb information like a sponge and do everything but talk. Let the other person know that's what you're doing."

HANK TRISLER

---

[2] David Stauffer. Yo, Listen Up: A Brief Hearing on the Most Neglected Communication Skill

8 Strategies for Active Listening

There are a number of strategies for becoming a better, more active listener.

1. Acknowledge that you could do better

Studies show that awareness alone is one of the greatest contributors to improved listening. "Some experts claim that 50% or more of the average adult's potential improvement in listening can come from realizing he or she has bad listening habits and is capable of listening much better."[3]

2. Practice Listening

Once you have established that you need to be a better listener, catch yourself out when you are not listening. By focusing on your listening activity, you begin to see listening as a conscious rather than an unconscious act. You are then in a better position to practice active listening skills and measure communication success.

Listening Fact #13

Leaders give good attention to the speaker by looking the speaker in the eye.

---

[3] Jack E. Hulbert. North Carolina A&T State University

Listening Fact #14

Leaders paraphrase the speaker to ensure understanding of the speaker's message.

3. Paraphrase to Ensure Understanding

Statements such as 'Is this what you are trying to tell me' and rephrase what you think the person would like to say, or 'what I hear you saying is…'.

Paraphrasing is an effective tool in demonstrating to the listener that you are trying to understand. It also enables the listener to make adjustments, corrections, or elaborations to the details to ensure accurate understanding.

4. Be aware of your talking habits

Become aware of how much talking you do compared with the other person.

If the conversation is one-sided this may tell you something about your listening skills. Keep the fight for 'air space' fair and ensure that both parties have an opportunity to contribute to the discussion.

5. Silence is Golden

The urge to fill a silence can be irresistible. However, we are best served by adopting a personal policy of not talking right away, no matter what another person says.

Even if you are asked a question for which you have a ready answer, take the time to think.

Something about the other person's tone of voice or the specific situation they describe, could be different from what you had imagined and may affect the quality of your answer.

The ability to pause is a true art in active listening.

6. Resolve not to let your mind wander

Listening Fact #15

If you are prone to drifting during a conversation because of something the speaker says, make a quick note to come back to your thoughts later.

Leaders are able to relate accurate messages to a third party, which shows that they listening to and remembered what the original speaker had said.

This makes it easier to stay in the 'here and now' and ensures that you resume paying attention.

"Leaders listen with an open mind by not becoming emotional or defensive."

ORICK, 2002

7. Take Notes

This communicates to the speaker that you really care about what they are saying and believe it is important enough to be recorded. It also keeps you occupied so you are less likely to interrupt or daydream. However in doing this, you need to ensure that the speaker knows you are genuinely listening. It is important to maintain rapport and engage with the speaker as you take notes.

8. Set the Scene

Avoid having important conversations in your office, where a busy desk, a ringing telephone, and emails, instant messages, or device notifications compete for your attention. Consider taking your conversation to a meeting room, or go outside for a walk. Not only is this good exercise, it provides an environment very free from distraction.

Complete Activity # 7
Quotable Quotes

ACTIVITY 7: QUOTABLE QUOTES

Throughout this Learning Short-take® a number of quotes about listening have been incorporated into your learning materials. Following are some additional quotes about listening.

Imagine for a moment that you are coaching a novice listener on the art of active listening. How would you explain each of these quotes in terms of their reference to active listening behaviors? List a couple of bullet points for each quote.

Quote 1: 'Wisdom is the reward you get for a lifetime of listening when you'd have preferred to talk.' - Doug Larson

Quote 2: 'Listen or thy tongue will keep thee deaf.' - Native American Indian Proverb

Quote 3: 'The most important thing in communication is to hear what isn't being said.' - Peter F. Drucker

Quote 4: 'Courage is what it takes to stand up and speak; courage is also what it takes to sit down and listen.' - Winston Churchill

Now update your Learning Journal (page 63)

"I know that you believe you understand what you think I said, but I'm not sure you realize that what you heard is not what I meant."

ROBERT MCCLOSKEY

TOP TIPS FOR EFFECTIVE LISTENING

PART 5

PART 5 - TOP TIPS FOR EFFECTIVE LISTENING

"The most important thing in communication is to hear what isn't being said."

PETER F. DRUCKER

- **Make time to listen.** Avoid looking at your watch or at other people or events going on around you. Use eye contact and listening body language. Face and lean toward the speaker and nod your head as appropriate.

- **Listen for what is not said.** Don't respond just to the meaning of the words; look for the feelings or intent beyond the words. Often the surface meaning of the words used by the sender is not the real message.

- **Keep your mind in the here and now.** Inhibit your tendency to mentally 'wander off'.

- **Set the scene for active listening.** Curb your impulse to immediately jump in and answer questions or give advice.

- **Paraphrase for understanding.** If you are confused and do not understand alert the speaker and ask them to re-phrase or clarify.

- **Know your listening style** and tune into the listening styles of others. Adapt your communication to suit. Be empathetic and non-judgmental. You can be accepting and respectful of the speaker and their feelings without invalidating or giving up your own position.
- **Be conscious of listening barriers** and seek to remove them where possible.
- **Don't interrupt.**
- **Make use of silence.**

 **Complete Activity # 8**
My Top Tips

 Download the **Listening Tips Job Aid** from https://www.catherinematttiske.com/books

ACTIVITY 8: MY TOP TIPS

Select your top 3 tips for effective listening and state how you will implement these into your work and daily life.

My top 3 tips are…	I will implement this tip by…
1.	
2.	
3.	

Now update your Learning Journal (page 63)

Section 2
LEARNING JOURNAL

The Learning Journal is used throughout the process to record your key learnings, hot tips and things to remember.

Update your Learning Journal at anytime. Ensure you complete your Learning Journal after you finish each activity. Then turn back to the Learning Short-take® to continue your learning.

LEARNING JOURNAL

As you work through this Learning Short-take®, make detailed notes on this page of the lessons you have learned and any useful skill areas. For each lesson or refresher point think about how you could further develop this skill. Your coach will want to discuss these with you in your Skill Development Action Planning meeting.

"…that is what learning is.
You suddenly understand something you've understood all your life, but in a new way."
DORIS LESSING

"Act as though it were impossible to fail. "
WINSTON CHURCHILL

> *"The wise do at once what the fool does later."*
> BALTASAR GRACIAN (1601-58), SPANISH JESUIT PRIEST AND AUTHOR.

Learning or Idea	Action to be taken	Result Expected

Learning Journal - continued

Learning or Idea	Action to be taken	Result Expected

"Anyone who stops learning is old, whether at twenty or eighty."
HENRY FORD

Learning or Idea	Action to be taken	Result Expected

"

"Wisdom is the reward you get for a lifetime of listening when you'd have preferred to talk."

DOUG LARSON

Section 3

SKILL DEVELOPMENT ACTION PLAN

Your Skill Development Action Plan is the last Step in the process. After you have completed the Learning Short-take® and all Activities, update your Learning Journal, then complete this section.

SKILL DEVELOPMENT ACTION PLAN

This is the most important part of the program - your individual Skill Development Action Plan.

You need to complete this plan before meeting with your manager or prior to on-going coaching. You will discuss it in detail with your manager or coach as he or she will ensure that you have everything you need to complete the tasks and activities.

Once you have completed your **Skill Development Action Plan** schedule a meeting time with your manager or coach to review your plan. Take your Learning Short-take® and all other documentation received during the training course to this meeting.

Remember - you have committed to your **Skill Development Action Plan**, and need to make time to complete your tasks!

> *"The mind, once stretched by a new idea, never regains its original dimensions."*
>
> OLIVER WENDELL HOLMES

> *"Whatever you can do or dream you can - begin it. Boldness has genius, power and magic."*
>
> JOHANN WOLFGANG VON GOETHE

"Imagination is the eye of the soul."
JOSEPH JOUBERT (1754-1824)

Task or activity (Be specific)	Measure (this will help you to know you have achieved it)	Date (Be specific)
Reflect on your Learning Journal. Transfer action items that you can apply to your job. Ensure that you include some 'stretch goals' and also a blend of short, medium and long term goals.	Apart from you, who else is needed to assist you in achieving your goal.	Be specific. A general date such as 'Quarter 1', 'August', or 'by end of year' is vague and more likely to result in not achieving your target. Be specific – e.g. 22nd November.

IDEAS FOR DISCUSSION WITH MY MANAGER

Ideas

CONGRATULATIONS!

You've now completed this Learning Short-take®.

Meet with your Manager/Coach to discuss your
Skill Development Action Plan.

"

"Courage is what it takes to stand up and speak; courage is also what it takes to sit down and listen."

WINSTON CHURCHILL

QUICK REFERENCE

This Quick Reference provides you with a summary of key concepts, models and reference material from Learning Short-takes®. We have also included some quotations to ponder.

Use this section as a quick reference to keep your learning active.

Quick Reference

Why Can't We Listen?

*Our brains are capable
of comprehending speech at four to five times
the rate at which most people can speak.
So as someone else is talking, we take all that
downtime and go out on mental excursions.*

JACK E. HULBERT

Listening versus Speaking

The average person talks at a rate of about 125 - 175 words per minute, while we can listen at a rate of up to 450 words per minute.

CARVER, JOHNSON, & FRIEDMAN, 1970

Quick Reference

The Business of Listening

Both business practitioners and academics listed listening as one of the most important skills for an effective professional, yet only 1.5% of articles in business journals dealt with listening effectiveness.

SMELTZER, 1993

Listening Barriers

When I ask you to listen to me and you start giving me advice, you have not done what I asked.
When I ask you to listen to me and you begin to tell me why I shouldn't feel that way, you are trampling on my feelings.
When I ask you to listen to me and you feel you have to do something to solve my problem, you have failed me - strange as that may seem.

LEO BUSCAGLIA

Quick Reference

Listening and Communication

Even the best communications are worthless if they fall on deaf ears.

RICHARD BIERCK

Listening and Memory

On average, viewers who just watched and listened to the evening news could only recall 17.2% of the content when not cued, and the cued group never exceeded 25%.

STAUFFER, FROST, & RYBOLT, 1983

Quick Reference

Selective Hearing

Two men were walking along a crowded sidewalk in a downtown business area. Suddenly one exclaimed, "Listen to the lovely sound of that cricket!"

But the other could not hear. He asked his companion how he could detect the sound of a cricket amidst the din of people and traffic. The first man, who was a zoologist, had trained himself to listen to the voices of nature, but he did not explain. He simply took a coin out of his pocket and dropped it on the sidewalk, whereupon a dozen people began to look about them. "We hear," he said, "what we listen for.

BHAGWAN SHREE RAJNEESH -
THE DISCIPLINE OF TRANSCENDENCE

Mehrabian's Model

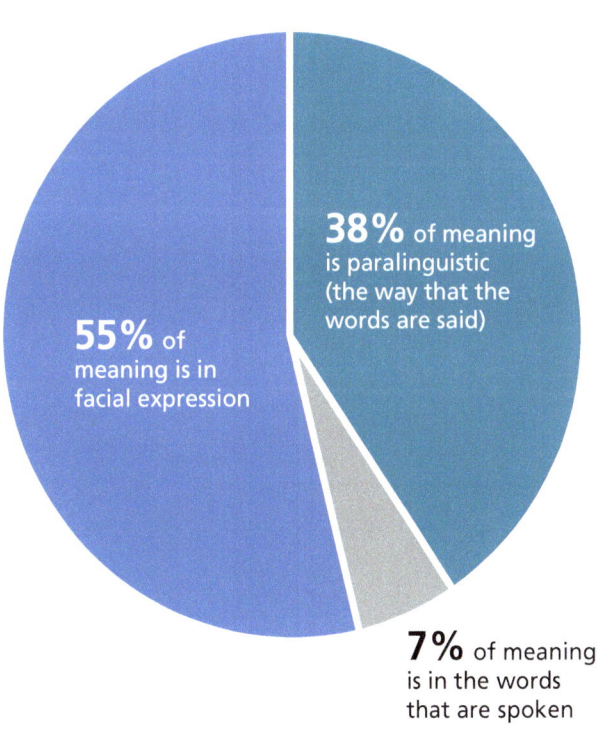

Quick Reference

Listening to Non-Verbal Communication

Spoken words only account for 30 -35% of the meaning. The rest is transmitted through nonverbal communication that only can be detected through visual and auditory listening.

BIRDWHISTELL, 1970

Using our Ears and our Mouths in Proportion

God gave us two ears but only one mouth. Some people say that's because he wanted us to spend twice as much time listening as talking. Other's claim it's because he knew listening was twice as hard as talking.

ANONYMOUS

Quick Reference

Listening Styles

People listen through one of four primary styles, including people oriented, time oriented, action oriented and content oriented.

Females are more likely to be people-oriented and males are more likely to be action, content, or time oriented.

BARKER & WATSON, 2000

Active Listening and Leadership

*Leaders paraphrase the speaker
to ensure understanding of the speaker's message.*

ORICK, 2002

*They are able to relate accurate messages to a third party,
which shows that they listening to
and remembered what the
original speaker had said.*

ORICK, 2002

"To listen well, is as powerful a means of influence as to talk well, and is as essential to all true conversation."

CHINESE PROVERB

NEXT STEPS

Congratulations! You have now completed this Learning Short-take® title. The entire list of Learning Short-takes® can be found on the catherinemattiske.com website.

In this section we have suggested Learning Short-take® titles for you that will build your learning. You may order these Learning Short-takes® online at https://www.catherinemattiske.com/books or from your bookstores.

Adult Learning Principles 1
Understanding the Ways Adults Learn

Learning Short-take® Outline

Adult Learning Principles 1 combines self-study with realistic workplace activities for trainers, educators, facilitators and managers to develop skills and knowledge in the principles of adult learning. It will add adult learning techniques to your 'grab bag' of learning design tools for improved learning outcomes. After evaluation of your current approach to learning design, you will learn to develop new and innovative strategies to engage learners at every level. Significantly increasing participant retention and training results **Adult Learning Principles 1** will fuel your confidence in designing successful training workshops and eLearning every time.

The principles of adult learning work on the basis that we all learn differently, and the way we like to receive and interpret information varies from person to person. Trainers and facilitators who use a combination of adult learning principles to provide balance in their programs increase the chances of keeping all participants focused and engaged throughout the learning process. **Adult Learning Principles 1** will assist you in building a good mix of adult learning styles which is critical in ensuring learning, thorough participant retention and workplace application.

Adult Learning Principles 1 includes the job aid Strategies for Meeting Global and Specific Needs, the **Adult Learning Principles Quick Reference Wall Chart** and the **Activity Booklet**, provided as free downloadable tools.

Learning Objectives

- Successfully match adult learning terms with definitions.
- Determine your personal Learning Style preference.
- List and give working examples of three Adult Learning Principles – Global vs Specific, Learning Styles and Learning Types.
- Develop strategies and ideas to link Adult Learning Principles with Instructional Design.

Course Content

- Part 1: Understanding Adult Learners
- Part 2: Adult Learning Principle 1 - Global vs Specific Learners
- Part 3: Adult Learning Principle 2 - Learning Style - Modalities
- Part 4: Adult Learning Principle 3 - Learning Types - The 4Mat System

Making Meetings Work
Getting the Most out of Meetings

Course Content

- Part 1: Types of Meetings
- Part 2: Why Meetings Fail
- Part 3: Solutions to Meeting Barriers
- Part 4: Planning the Meeting
- Part 5: Preparing the Agenda
- Part 6: Conducting the Meeting

Learning Short-take® Outline

Making Meetings Work combines self-study with realistic workplace activities to provide you with the key skills and techniques to make meetings work. Your meetings will become more focused, efficient, targeted and more likely to have a productive impact on the company's bottom-line. You will learn how to more effectively prepare, manage, facilitate and actively participate in meetings.

It is estimated that the average professional spends 61.5 hours per month in meetings, or two weeks every year. It is also estimated that at least 50% of this time is wasted in unproductive meeting activity. **Making Meetings Work** will provide you with the tools to help you save time and money.

Making Meetings Work includes the **Meeting Administration Checklist, Meeting Agenda** and **Meeting Minutes** provided as free downloadable tools.

Learning Objectives

- Evaluate your current level of meeting success.
- Identify the various types of meetings and explain key differences.
- Develop solutions to common meeting problems.
- Outline the steps for a successful meeting.
- Carry out meeting planning and preparation.
- Create a Skill Development Action Plan.

Influencing for Opportunity
Identify and Maximize Ways to Influence

Course Content

- Part 1: Fundamentals of Influence
- Part 2: Influence: A Choice
- Part 3: Naturally Occurring Influence Patterns
- Part 4: Methods of Persuasion
- Part 5: The Challenges of Influence
- Part 6: Building a life of Influence

Learning Short-take® Outline

Influencing for Opportunity combines self-study with realistic workplace activities to provide you with the key skills and techniques to influence those around you. You will learn the theory of influence, influence principles and strategies, as well as how to plan and prepare for important opportunities to influence. As a result, you should achieve greater results in your organization, work more productively and effectively in a team environment, and develop stronger working relationships with co-workers, suppliers and customers.

The ability to influence others is critical in today's competitive business environment. Being highly skilled in influence enables you to build the relationships you need to get results inside or outside the organization. Employees and managers alike cannot assume they have power over others - they must earn it through influence. Being an influential person is a skill that can be learned and practiced. **Influencing for Opportunity** will help you succeed in the modern corporate environment by increasing your ability to influence others.

Influencing for Opportunity includes a **toolkit of job aids and learning support tools** provided to you as free downloads.

Learning Objectives

- Identify patterns of influence.
- Evaluate how you currently use influence behaviors and identify areas for development.
- Develop influence behaviors for greater personal and business success.
- Establish clear and powerful influence goals.
- Increase influence to overcome resistance.
- Describe how to ask for and receive support.
- Design an approach for formal and informal influence situations; apply the approach to a real-life situation.
- Create a Skill Development Action Plan.

www.catherinemattiske.com

www.ingramcontent.com/pod-product-compliance
Lightning Source LLC
Chambersburg PA
CBHW040002110526
44587CB00001BA/21